The Ultimate Guide to Running a Counselor & Leaders in Training Program for Teens: Lesson Plans, Activities, Projects, & More

Copyright © 2021 by Beechtree Assets, LLC Luke Bouma Owner.

Beechtree Assets, LLC
Feedback@Beechtreeassets.com
www.BeechtreeAssets.com

Ordering Information:
Quantity sales. Special discounts are available on quantity purchases by corporations, associations, and others. For details, contact the publisher at the email address above.
Orders by U.S. trade bookstores and wholesalers. Please contact Feedback@Beechtreeassets.com

Printed in the United States of America

Introduction

Leaders aren't born, they are made. And they are made just like anything else, through hard work. And that's the price we'll have to pay to achieve that goal, or any goal.
—Vince Lombardi

When I was in my teens, I was fortunate enough to participate in a Leaders in Training program at a camp in Maine. This program gave me the foundation I needed for college and later when I started several successful companies. The skills I learned through that leadership program have helped me become the person I am today both professionally and personally.

Two important but difficult programs run by camps are the Counselors in Training (CIT) and Leaders in Training (LIT) programs. Finding staff to implement an effective CIT/LIT program can be extremely difficult as program staff struggle to run all the other aspects of camp. Increasingly, campers desire to become leaders and demands for CIT/LIT programs are growing across the United States. According to a survey from WorkplaceTrends.com and Virtuali called "The Millennial Leadership Study," more than 90% of millennials aspire to become leaders but many of them lack the skills they need. Sadly, we are raising youth who want to lead, but we are not giving them the tools they need to do so. My hope in writing this book is to offer camps an easy-to-use resource that will help staff teach the next generation of leaders.

As with all skills, it is important that leaders work to refine their leadership skills. No one is born a great leader. Every effective leader must work at developing their leadership skills. Without that hard work, you can only be an average leader at best. We hope that this book helps you teach your campers to become great leaders.

Camps often lack an easy-to-use program for the staff running the CIT/LIT programs. This can result in CITs and LITs being treated as cheap labor. Or the program becomes just a way to keep campers coming back until they can become counselors. By doing so, many campers are robbed of a life changing growth opportunity and camps are hurting their chances of attracting paying campers.

This program will help you train the next generation of great leaders no matter who you have running your CIT/ LIT program. They will not only be able to train youth to become effective camp counselors next year but contributing members of society soon and even successful CEOs or inventors in ten years. To do that, this program focuses on giving the campers skills they can use no matter where life takes them.

The Ultimate Guide to Running a Counselor & Leaders in Training Program for Teens is a program that can easily be adapted to any already existing camp program whether it is a week-long or ten weeks. With a long list of activities, projects, and lesson plans, this resource has all you need to run a successful CIT/LIT camp program except the personnel.

No matter what your goal is with your CIT/ LIT program, this book can help you give your campers a life changing experience while you mold the best possible future counselors for your camp.

How This Program Works

This Counselors in Training (CIT) and Leaders in Training (LIT) program's structure is set up for ten weeks of activities to teach campers leadership skills. You do not need to do all ten weeks. If your camp is a weekly camp, there is a program for that. If you have a two-week, four-week, or eight-week program, for example, just pick the weeks and activities you would like to use from this book. Asterisks * are next to the most important activities.

Each week has five days of activities covering three hours: one hour of daily classroom instruction on leadership skills, one hour of physical activities to teach leadership, and one optional hour for campers to work on their projects or perform community service. Adjust these activities to fit your camp needs.

Suggested Daily Schedule

The suggested daily schedule consists of one hour of "classroom" instruction in the morning covering leadership basics.

In the afternoon, following lunch and rest time, spend one hour on a physical game/activity as found in the back of this book. Afterward, campers can spend one hour working on projects or community service.

Again, adjust these activities to fit your needs.

Yearly Team Project

We strongly encourage you to include a big project for your campers to work on as a large group or in smaller teams. The project could be something like planning a massive camp activity, such as the color war, or a series of smaller camp activities. Doing both as a weekly activity gives different campers an opportunity to lead.

Camper Burn Out

For campers, this may be the first time they are put under real stress as they handle projects and absorb high level leadership and teamwork material.

Remember: We want them to learn from this and not for it to be so hard they stop enjoying and learning.

Give campers days off to do fun activities. We set this program up as a five-day-per-week class. This means two days a week they can do other stuff or take a day off. I recommend not giving back-to-back days off because we want the youth to maintain the CIT/LIT program mindset.

Consider building a CIT/LIT lounge if you offer an overnight program. The youth should have their own area to relax in, but it is also an area they can still be supervised in.

Having their own days off and break areas reinforces that these young leaders are special and attracts new campers to the CIT/LIT program when they become older.

Remember: The youth are still teenagers. Make sure they are getting the physical and mental rest they need.

Community Service

We encourage you to put a few hours aside each week for community service. Typically, community service is performed later in the week or camp session. Service can be done around camp, such as cleaning up an area or creating a new campsite for overnights, or in the community, such as working a few hours a week at a local food pantry.

Volunteering at camp or in the community builds team and community pride. It also teaches the youth what real work is like.

Projects

A major part of this program is projects. Nothing is better at leadership training than giving the youth hands-on opportunities to lead. In this section, we offer an overview of our ideal project program and some suggested projects. During this program we will have both weekly projects and a program-long (big) project. Adjust these to your program.

Example Weekly Projects

- Planning and leading an end of week activity
- Running an evening activity
- Coordinating a special themed day

Example Program-Long Projects

- Running end of camp color war
- Throwing a final camp-wide party
- Leading closing camp ceremonies
- Completing a campgrounds project
- Coordinating a post-camp party for staff

Suggestions

Not all your campers need to work on the same project. Assign the campers to multiple project teams. This gives more campers an opportunity to take on leadership roles. Consider rotating leaders assigned to weekly projects.

How the Project Works

After being assigned to a project, the campers are responsible for running as much of the big project as possible.

Phase 1: Ideas

The first part should take about one-third of the time you have for camp. Campers should create a presentation for how they want to run the activity. They need to clearly lay out what they want to do, how it will run, and any costs. Campers must give a presentation to you for approval. The exact format is up to you, but the presentation should clearly explain all aspects of the project.

Phase 2: Detailed Plans & Preparation

Planning and preparation should take about one-third of the time campers have. During this part, the campers should work on the approved project. They should plan every aspect of the project from start to finish including procuring any needed materials. Meetings with other staff, trips to the store, and any extras should happen during this step. At the end of the project, the leaders should present a project update to you so you can make sure everything is on track.

Phase 3: Finalizing the Project

Putting the finishing touches on their big projects should take up the final one-third of their stay. During this phase, campers should still be running their projects. Have them hold a final meeting right before the campers lead the project to ensure everyone is on the same page. This also helps them get experience running meetings.

Final Thoughts about the Project

At the end of each project meet with the campers as a group and review how it went. If you had assigned leaders, meet with them one-on-one in a public area.

Give them twice as much positive feedback than criticism. Be honest with them and be careful how you give feedback. We want the campers to get better and sometimes that means you need to be kindly blunt.

Make sure that they create their presentations at each step. This helps them learn public speaking and to clearly put their ideas into words.

Our goal is to give the campers real-world leadership and public speaking experience. The ability to speak in front of others and communicate ideas is crucial in many walks of life, but especially for leaders. This is a skill you need to develop because few people naturally enjoy or are good at public speaking.

Suggestions

The goal is to not only teach the campers leadership ideas but also to help them put these skills into practice. To teach teens to be better leaders, you need to give them hands-on leadership opportunities not just in-class lectures.

Focus on the big picture of teaching them but also give them tasks and responsibilities to help them learn from what they have been taught. That is where projects come in.

The Most Important Part: The Projects

Teaching someone how to do something can only go so far. If you want to help them become real leaders, they need opportunities to have responsibilities and make decisions. Giving campers projects to work on should be a focus of your CIT/LIT program.

This program has three project focuses. The first is to create and manage activities throughout the camp year. These can be evening programs or leading an activity like soccer. The campers must create a plan and implement it. This can be done as a large group or several smaller groups.

The second focus is service projects in your community or at your camp. Service helps campers get out into the community and bond with it and their teammates.

The third focus is the massive group project. Many camps use CITs to help with a big final color war or similar event. Consider having your campers work with camp staff to plan part or all of an activity. Then have them oversee setting up the all-camp obstacle course or act as judges during an event. Give them responsibility in a safe, supervised way that will help them put what they have learned into practice.

Give an hour every day for campers to work on these projects. Before you move on to the Lesson Plans section, think about what projects your campers can do that will help them learn by doing.

Lesson Plans

Leaders aren't born, they are made. And they are made just like anything else, through hard work. And that's the price we'll have to pay to achieve that goal, or any goal.
—Vince Lombardi

The following are ten weeks of lesson plans for your camp's CIT/LIT program. We also include, at the end, a one-week program for anyone who has a single week to run a CIT program. You can take these lesson plans and use them in any order you want. Have a shorter program? Cut some of the classes that you do not have time for. An asterisk * is next to the most important lessons.

Remember: Give campers the skills and practice they need to become leaders.

Each of these ten week-long programs are broken into five days' worth of lessons. If you need additional days, pull from other weeks. Each of these daily lesson plans are designed to run for three one-hour blocks per day.

Week 1

Day 1: Introduction, Expectations, & Goal Setting*

Day 2: What It Means to Be a Leader

Day 3: Overcoming Difficulties

Day 4: Improving Communication*

Day 5: Modeling a Leader

Week 2

Day 1: The Traps of Bad Leadership*

Day 2: The Dangers of Groupthink

Day 3: The Dangers of Money

Day 4: Evaluations

Day 5: Building Respect

Week 3

Day 1: Practicing Communication*

Day 2: Presentations

Day 3: Presentations: Part 2

Day 4: Social Media

Day 5: Self-Care

Week 4

Day 1: Seeing What & Where You Are Leading

Day 2: Dealing with Burn Out

Day 3: The Dangers of Scapegoating

Day 4: The Power of Brainstorming & Diversity

Day 5: Brainstorming

Week 5

Day 1: Practicing Communication Again*

Day 2: Presentations

Day 3: Presentations: Part 2

Day 4: Setting Realistic Goals

Day 5: Goal Presentations

Week 6

Day 1: Evaluations*

Day 2: Evaluations & Community Service Projects

Day 3: Building Your Resume

Day 4: Interviewing Tips & Practice

Day 5: Community Service

Week 7

Days 1–3: Interviews*

Day 4: Treating Others with Respect

Day 5: Project Day

Week 8

Day 1: How to Be a Better Listener*

Days 2–4: Camp Internships

Day 5: Internship Recap

Week 9

Days 1–3: What If Activities

Days 4–5: Preparing for the Final Push

Week 10: Closing Week

Days 1–2: Final Projects*

Day 3: Wrapping Up

Day 4: Closing Ceremonies & Party

Day 5: Goodbye

Week 1

Become the kind of leader that people would follow voluntarily; even if you had no title or position.
—Brian Tracy

Welcome to the first week of the CIT/LIT program. The goal at the start of this program no matter if it's a week or a single day should be to explain what will be expected from the campers, set some goals, and lay a foundation of information they can use to become leaders.

Day 1: Introduction, Expectations, & Goal Setting*

Today we are going to welcome the campers and not only introduce them to the program but also try to get them excited for what is to come. Do your best to make this as fun as possible for the campers so they are excited to give it their all.

Hour 1: Classroom Instruction

Take the first hour of classroom instruction to clearly explain what is expected from your campers. Ask them what they expect from the program and from you as the leader.

If your campers have yet to meet each other, keep the getting to know you part of the introduction to a minimum and save it for the games/activities hour later in the day.

Talk about goals and the importance of goals to help complete tasks in a timely manner. Give each of your campers a pocket-size notebook. Tell them to write down three goals each night for the following day. These goals must not be everyday tasks, such as getting dressed or eating. Instead, they should focus on tasks they want to get done, such as asking a question in class or completing a task for their project. If yours is a weekly program, have them also write down three weekly goals. Let them know that you will be randomly asking them to show their notebooks to you and explain their goals for the day or week.

Questions for Campers

- What is a goal?
- What are some daily goals you should set each night?
- What are some weekly goals that will challenge you?

Hour 2: Games/Activities

After your break from classroom learning, set up an activity that can serve as a Day 1 ice breaker.

Consider using an activity from our activity list that focuses on team building to help the campers start to bond, such as the group logo activity.

Hour 3: Project Time

In this hour, clearly explain what projects the campers will be working on. With this being the first week of a one-week or a multiweek camp, start with a simple week-long project. For example, taking charge of an upcoming evening activity or leading an activity period for a small group of campers with the help of camp staff.

If yours is a multiweek camp and has a bigger project the campers will be working on, talk to them about it but let them know you will be starting it in the days to come. It is smart to give the campers an easy project before they get to work on a larger, more difficult, project.

A leader is defined as someone who can make a decision and is responsible for it, but there is so much more to being a leader.

Inform your campers that in the future this hour will be used for project work. They will also likely need to find time outside of this hour to work on the projects if they hope to complete them on time.

Day 2: What It Means to Be a Leader

So, you want to be a leader? Well, what does that mean? Today we are going to give the campers a good idea what being a leader really means.

Hour 1: Classroom Instruction

When teaching how to be a leader it is important to help campers learn what it means to be a leader. We often think of skills and personalities we see in good leaders. Keep this short, but get their minds working on what it means to be a good leader.

In this class we will cover five must-have leadership skills. (There are more, but to keep it to an hour we focus on five.)

- Integrity & Respect

- Ability to Delegate
- Effective Communicator
- Aware
- Lifelong Learner

Integrity & Respect

If you are to be a leader you need the respect of others. To do this, you need to have integrity and respect for others. According to the *Oxford Dictionary* integrity is the "quality of being honest and having strong moral principles; moral uprightness." If you do not have integrity or respect the people you are leading, they will not respect you as a leader. If you do not have integrity in the way you treat people, and you do not follow through on what you say, how can people trust you to lead them?

Ability to Delegate

As a leader you cannot do it all! Otherwise, you would not be a leader but a hard worker. As a leader you need to build a team of people you can trust to complete part of the job so that the big picture task can be completed.

Effective Communicator

As a leader you must learn how to clearly communicate with all types of people from employees to customers to government officials to board members. You will need to clearly give all types of information including instruction and feedback. Ask your campers how frustrating a homework assignment is when the teacher does not clearly explain the expectations. Use that as an example of why it is important to clearly communicate.

Aware

This one is often overlooked by leaders, but if you are not aware of what is happening around you how can you lead people through it? A good leader needs to be focused on what is happening around them and how their team is responding to it so they can lead their team through it.

Continuous Learner

It is easy in this fast-changing world to become stale and outdated. History is full of what was once a popular business that failed to adapt to new changes and died out. A leader must keep learning new things so they can keep their company moving forward.

Questions for Campers

- Which one of these skills do you consider to be the most important and why?
- Which skill do you excel at?
- Which skill do you need to work on improving?

Hour 2: Games/Activities

Consider using one of our activities that looks at what it means to be a leader like the I Am Leader game or the What Leaders Do You Respect? activity to reinforce these five leadership skills.

Hour 3: Project Time

Use this hour to let your campers actively work on their Week 1 project. As this is the first hour of free work, guide them in areas they should be working on. If this is a multiweek camp, start thinking about how to get the campers working on the larger project. Do they need to be broken into smaller groups? Is there someone you want to assign to be a leader of the project or parts of the project?

Day 3: Overcoming Difficulties

Anyone can hold the helm when the sea is calm.
—Publilius Syrus

Life is filled with difficulties. It's important to learn how to respond. The most successful people in the world have repeatedly hit difficulty in one form or another. Sometimes the difference between a successful project and a failed one is how the leader responds to difficulty.

Success is the ability to go from one failure to another with no loss of enthusiasm.
—Winston Churchill

Hour 1: Classroom Instruction

Most of us have faced difficulty at some point in our lives. Being successful as a leader often comes down to how you overcome difficulties.

Ask what difficulties the campers have had to overcome. After taking a few, ask your campers about difficulties a leader might face. Keep it short. Just take a few answers.

Tips to Overcoming Challenges

The following are a few tips to help you overcome challenges.

Do Not Give Up

Way too often people hit a roadblock and stop with minimal effort to overcome their challenges. While sometimes you truly cannot overcome issues with a project and need to make major changes do not walk away until you have really given it a hard look.

Thomas Edison tried a thousand times to find the correct balance to make the first light bulb before it worked. Sometimes you just need to keep trying in life and as a leader as that can be the difference between being successful and giving up and failing a project.

Look at the Big Picture

When we hit a roadblock, it is easy to become focused on that issue and forget the big picture. Consider stepping back and looking at the big picture before trying to figure out the issues.

There was once a company that made drill bits. After years of struggling to grow the company, the owner switched his thinking from how to make drill bits to how to make holes. The company started manufacturing different devices to make holes. With this new focus, they found new customers and quickly grew because they looked at the big picture not the small problem.

Get Help

As a leader you need to know when to ask for help. Talking with someone who has been there before or someone with a different point of view can help you find new ideas. Reading a wide variety of materials can give you new ideas and different perspectives as well.

Accept the Obstacle

We often are focused on defeating the issues in our path that we do not learn to accept them and find a way to incorporate them into our plans. Maybe you did not get the exact teammate, roommate, or venue you wanted but what you did get likely has its own benefits if you take the time to look at it.

Questions for Campers

- What obstacles are most common as a leader?
- What do you do when you face an obstacle?
- What could you do in the future?

Hour 2: Games/Activities

Consider doing an activity to problem solve as a team, such as the group logo activity or the What If game found in the included activity section of the book.

Hour 3: Project Time

Touch base with the campers during the free hour to work on their project. Talk about the deadline for the week's project and help them measure whether they will reach the goal.

Do not be afraid of giving advice but avoid doing the work for them.

Day 4: Improving Communication*

Today, there are more ways than ever to communicate with people and, at the same time, communication can be harder than ever. Increasingly we are not all in the same room, building, or even city or country. Being able to communicate clearly both in writing and verbally can help you become a stronger leader.

Hour 1: Classroom Instruction

In today's instruction we give tips on how to clearly communicate as a leader and in everyday life.

Improving Communication

Ask if any campers have ever experienced a time when someone's instructions were not clear. Offer an example of a time in your life when you had the same issue. Ask them what their preferred method of communication is. Writing? A phone call? Face to face? Point out how different campers have different communication preferences.

Communicate Both in Writing and Verbally

Not everyone learns the same way. Some people are audible learners; others need it in writing. As a leader, it is important to not only tell your team something but to also put it clearly in writing so they can look it over again in the future.

Remember: Put important information both in writing and verbally to make sure there is no confusion.

Be Clear and Concise

As a leader one of the best things to do when giving direction and instruction is to be clear and concise. We can confuse people by dragging out conversations instead of getting to the point. When you are making an announcement or giving instructions be brief and clear. Edit your work.

When conversations go long, consider sending a follow-up email breaking down the key points.

Make Eye Contact

Whenever you are talking in front of a group of people or even one on one, making eye contact is crucial. It will not only build credibility in what you are saying but making eye contact also keeps listeners focused on what you are saying. Plus, you can tell if people are listening if they are looking back at you.

If you are in a group, make eye contact for short moments with as many people as possible.

Respect Your Audience

Sometimes it can be easy to talk down to an audience by not really understanding who you are talking to. If this is an audience that is highly educated on the topic it can be rude to talk to them as if they are brand new. Or if they are new it can be rude to talk to them as if they are experts using terms they do not know. Be respectful of the people you are talking with and take the time to learn about them before you talk with them.

Double Check

Do your best to communicate accurate information. Mistakes happen, but repeatedly telling your staff incorrect information is a quick way to lose trust. Double check everything you communicate, especially when it is in writing.

When You Have to Say No, Explain Why

Often, we as leaders have to say no to a team member. It is important to also say why you are saying no. A straight-out no is often seen as an attack, but a carefully explained no can help avoid hard feelings. Be as positive as possible when saying no, but do not leave the door open to a future yes if you have no plans to do so. That will only lead to long-term hard feelings.

Hour 2: Games/Activities

In the five-day program, the first project is due tomorrow. You can use this hour to run an activity or give them free work to make sure they are set up for their first weekly project for tomorrow.

Hour 3: Project Time

At the start of the hour touch base with the campers and ask them what still needs to be done before the next day's activities. Make sure that they are on track by giving tips and suggestions if they ask.

Day 5: Modeling a Leader

With leadership you often must present yourself as a leader even when you do not feel like a leader. It's similar to the way an actor presents themselves in a role. As a leader you must act in a way that uses the skills you learned in the CIT/LIT program. Today we will explore how to act as a leader even when you do not feel like you are one.

Hour 1: Becoming the Leader

At the start of class consider reading a short speech once in a shy, stumbling way and once in a confident, clear way. Use this as an example to your campers. We want to convey the idea that you can act like a leader even when you do not feel like a leader.

Bring up examples of how as campers get ready to lead their project in front of other campers they act as a leader.

Talk to your campers about thinking of what they want from a leader and taking on those traits. Remember you can be a different person at home but at the workplace you always need to be a leader.

Questions for Campers

- Do you think your teachers act the same way at home as they do at school? Why?
- Do you think a boss is the same person with their family as they are with their team? Why?
- Give an example of a time when you acted not yourself to get through a situation.

Hour 2: Free Work Time

Let campers use the usual games/activities time to prepare to lead their project. You can also talk with them and go over everything they learned. Make sure they are set up for success.

Hour 3: The Big Project

In this hour CIT/LIT campers should lead their project with campers around camp. This may be a daytime class or a nighttime activity.

After the projects are completed, touch base with the campers as a group and review how it went. Meet with them one on one if needed to give both positive feedback and constructive criticism.

Week 2

He who has never learned to obey cannot be a good commander.
—Aristotle

Now that we introduced them to the program and started with some basics lets dive deeper into what it means to be a leader. Build on what you have already done as we examine how to become a great leader.

Day 1: The Traps of Bad Leadership*

If all we do is talk about how to be a good leader and we do not warn the campers of what makes a bad leader it can be easy to fall into a trap. Today we go over the traits of a bad leader to help campers avoid becoming one.

Hour 1: Classroom Instruction

We all have had a bad boss or a bad teacher. What made them this way, and how can we avoid becoming one? Talk with your campers about any experiences you may have had with a bad leader and go over the top pitfalls leaders fall into.

Communication

You can be the nicest boss and best leader ever but if you do not effectively communicate with your team the work will not be accomplished. We already talked about what makes a good communicator but remember lack of communication can be the main way good leaders turn bad.

Micromanaging

As a leader it is tempting to just do it yourself or stand over your employees as they work removing their ability to think and act on their own. Learn to trust your team because they are not robots. You need to train them and let them do their jobs.

Micromanaging can also mean you are so busy focusing on one small part that you lose focus of the big picture. A leader must always be focused on making sure everything is moving in the same direction not just on one part of it.

Favorites

One of the best ways to destroy a team is to have a favorite. When one person is treated better than others it can quickly build resentment within the team. This one is easy to fall into because when you find someone who is capable you often keep giving them work. This runs the risk of burning them out and making others feel like you do not respect them.

Make sure to treat all employees equally. Respect all of them and be careful about picking favorites even when you do not mean to.

Being a Bully

Some people may think it is easier to get work done by bullying or tearing someone down when a mistake happens instead of building them up. Work hard to build people up because a team that gets built up will be a team that works far harder than a team that is being torn down by a bully of a leader.

Vision and a Plan

You cannot be a leader if you are just responding to what is happening around you. A leader needs to have a plan and a vision of where they want to go as a team. I highly encourage you to not only have a plan and vision but a plan and vision your team knows and is working together toward.

Being a Know-It-All

One of the biggest traps any successful leader can fall into is this idea that they are clearly better than others. It is easy after finding success to say *I must just be smarter or better than all the others around me*. Great leaders who fall into this trap suddenly stop accepting help from others and miss out on exceptional ideas that others may come up with.

Also, when you act as the powerful know-it-all your team members will stop thinking for themselves resulting in a situation we call groupthink where people stop thinking and just act because they think that is what the leader wants.

Questions for Campers

- Which one of these traps of bad leadership do you think is most easily fallen into?
- Have you ever fallen victim to one of these traps?
- Do you know a good leader who did?

Hour 2: Games/Activities

Consider adding a team building/leadership game like The Puzzle, Ball Maze, or Team Jump Rope found in the activity section.

Hour 3

If you still have plenty of time for the big end of the season project consider breaking your campers into smaller teams with week-long projects. Assign a leader to each project. Keep the teams small so each week you can rotate project leaders.

If you are running low on time consider getting all the campers to focus on the big end of the season project.

Day 2: The Dangers of Groupthink

Groupthink has been the downfall of both companies and nations. With groupthink everyone blindly assumes that what they are doing is right and the group mindset can force people to ignore important information that contradicts what the group thinks is right. This can happen when a leader makes his wishes known and his team does their best to meet his goals even when there are clear dangers to his plan. Groupthink can also force many who have concerns to think they are in the minority, so they stay quiet. But they are really in the majority, and they are unwilling to speak up, so they never find out what they think is right.

Ask yourself how many times in your life have you just accepted what your friends or family tell you without looking into it? It is easy to just accept ideas from people you respect instead of analyzing it yourself.

Today we are going to talk about what groupthink is and how we can avoid it.

Hour 1: Classroom Instruction

During this class we are going to look at the dangers of groupthink both to the organization and to the leader.

Often we continue down a path as a team when it clearly will not work because we do not want to be the person to stand up to a large group of people and say this is wrong. We also often do it because we like the leader we are working for and want to find a way to make her happy.

A leader who has created a culture where no one is willing to speak up has created a ticking bomb that will someday blow up.

It is important that a leader create a culture that allows people to speak up and even encourages them to do so when they do not agree with the leader. This enables people to bring up honest concerns even when it seems they are the only one thinking them.

Groupthink can also lead to lack of creativity because no one is willing to bring up new ideas.

How groupthink happens:

- A leader refuses to listen to others.
- A leader makes his wishes known even when that leader has not thoroughly researched the topic.
- A culture where the group and the team are always right and can do no wrong has been created. This leads many to not want to speak up when they see something wrong.
- Removing anyone from the group who does not 100% support the leader can often lead to the rest of the group being unwilling to speak out.

How to prevent groupthink and get fresh ideas:

- A leader should avoid giving their opinion early on when trying to address an issue or assigning projects. Give staff the time they need to come up with their own ideas.
- Make it clear you want someone to be the "devil's advocate" and give you negative feedback on an idea or plan.
- The leader should remain critical and encourage team members to also always be asking why and if there is a better way.
- Reward people who get creative and speak their mind. This encourages others to do the same.
- Seek a diverse group of team members to get unique ideas and points of view.

Questions for Campers

- How dangerous do you think groupthink can be at work and at home?
- Have you ever fallen for groupthink?
- How do you plan to ensure your team members know they can speak up?

Hour 2: Games/Activities

Give campers an opportunity to speak their own point of view by doing an activity that forces them as a group to work out the problems. The Puzzle game in our activities list not only makes them work on their own but forces them to think as a group to put the complete puzzle together.

Hour 3: Project Time

Consider having some small group meetings to talk about the larger project and encourage them to look at the big picture. Encourage the groups working on the weekly project to step up their game this week.

Day 3: The Dangers of Money

In college you can learn all about how to manage money and create reports, but we want to talk about how important being a good steward of money is.

One of the number one reasons commanders in the US Army are relieved of command is the misuse of money. This often falls under failure to properly track how the money is being spent and spending it in ways that were not approved.

Today we are going to explore the responsibility and the dangers of working with other people's money. The goal is to teach campers to have a healthy respect for the responsibilities that come with being a leader.

If you can, give campers a small budget of money to spend on their big project or a weekly project. Maybe it is just a little pocket money or more to buy supplies depending on what they are working on. Force them as a team to decide how to spend the money and explain that they will have to justify how they spent the money later.

Hour 1: The Dangers of Money & Leadership

As a leader you will often be put in charge of other people's money. In this hour we are going to examine how a leader needs to take responsibility for the money related to a project. We will also address the keys to taking care of other people's money. And we will touch on how to take care of your money when you own a company.

Keys to Taking Care of Other People's Money

So, someone is trusting you take care of their money. That is a huge responsibility and one of the main reasons people get fired is misuse of money.

Treat It as Your Own

When you are responsible for other people's money you need to treat it as if it were your own. If you fail to properly take care of it and lose it or misuse it you may be forced to pay it back. Make sure to account for how you spent the money and take good care of it.

Account for Every Penny

When you oversee money, you need to be able to account for all of it. Failure to account for money can easily result in the owner of the money assuming you squandered it all. Keep receipts and track why it was spent not just where you spent the money.

Secure the Money

When in charge of other people's money, you must ensure that you are accountable for how it was spent but also how it is stored. You do not want to find yourself explaining how the money was stolen or misused by others.

Managing Money as an Owner

Some day you may own your own company. This puts even more pressure on you to track every penny you spend.

How to Manage Money When You Are the Owner

There are a few keys to managing money when you are the owner of the company.

Keep Your Personal Money and Work Money Separate

It is important when you own a company that your personal and work money are kept separate. This will make paying taxes easier and protect your personal money and assets if you ever get sued.

It is important to properly separate your money, or the IRS and others will start paying attention. When you start a company, get a professional accountant to help you.

Track Your Money

Sometimes when it is your money it is easy to stop thinking about how you are going to track it. As an owner it is even more important that you can track every penny so when the IRS knocks wanting you to explain everything you can.

There are many great software programs to track your spending. Use one and get a professional accountant too.

Pay Your Taxes

Did you know one of the main reasons for divorce is failure to pay taxes leading to huge fees and fines?

Some business owners will try not to fully report all income, or they try not to pay all of their taxes in an effort to save money. The IRS is good at finding people who are not paying all their taxes and fining them. This has forced many profitable companies to close because they are suddenly hit with massive fines on back taxes. This forces the owner to sell off what they own or to sell the company to pay off taxes that would have been a lot cheaper if they had just paid them on time.

Tip: If you own a company, hire a professional accountant to handle your money.

Hour 2: Games/Activities

If you can, have the campers look at their project budget. Then have them come up with an outline of how they plan to spend the money and when.

If money is not part of your program, consider having them use fake money or practice in a game like This or That? found in the suggested activities. Campers get a limited amount of money—not enough to buy everything they want—and need to as a team decide which items are most important. Toy money can be a great tool for this game.

Hour 3: Free Work

Before the campers are sent on their way for free work touch base with them. Make sure they are on time for what they need to do and offer a few tips and suggestions on how they can improve their projects.

Day 4: Evaluations

Taking an honest look at yourself is hard but having others examine you can be even harder. What may surprise people is how difficult it is to give a good, honest evaluation of your team members.

Today we are going to cover how to evaluate team members you are responsible for with constructive feedback. We are also going to start one-on-one evaluations of each of the campers in the CIT/LIT program.

Hour 1: Classroom Instruction

There are three main areas that every leader must evaluate team members on. We will look at them and give tips on how do an evaluation.

Before you start it is important to do your research. Learn what your team does, so you can effectively evaluate them. Make sure you make notes and have what you want to say clear before you meet with them. Nothing will lose you the respect of your team members like appearing to have no idea what they do.

When you give feedback, take time to listen to your staff and give them an opportunity to respond. You may learn something important, and they will respect you for taking the time to listen to them.

Make sure to compliment them more than you make suggestions for areas to improve. This helps campers feel good about the evaluation and more willing to improve.

Quality of Work and Taking Ownership

We all understand that quality of work is someone doing a good job, but what about initiative? Do you as a leader need to walk them step by step through everything or do they act before they are told when dealing with any issues that come up in their area of work?

Talk with your staff about areas to improve and, more importantly, areas they are excelling at.

Being on Time & on Budget

Being on time has many meanings like showing up to work on time (which is actually showing up early). Yet one of the most important tasks for an employee is to get projects done on time/on schedule/before a deadline. If one person is always late it can slow down the team as they wait for that one person to get their work done. Take this time to look at how your campers are doing with their timelines. Also talk to them about setting up honest and reachable goals.

Working as a Team

We all have that time where we wished we could do a project all by ourselves, but the truth is that is not possible. You must work as a team, and how you do it is important. Talk with your staff about how they are a good member of the team and how they are working with other members handling any issues in the team.

Final Notes

Give feedback sandwich style: I highly suggest always starting with some positive feedback, moving to an area to improve on, and wrapping up with a positive area.

End by telling your campers you will be meeting with each of them to discuss their progress.

Hour 2: One-On-One Evaluations

During this hour start the one-on-one evaluations. They should be ten minutes each. Make sure to do them in a public area where others can see you. The other campers can work on their projects during this time.

Hour 3: Free Work Time

Finish any one-on-one meetings. If you need more time, find it outside of the class time.

Day 5: Building Respect

We all want to be respected. Even if you do not want to be loved as a leader you want to be respected as a leader. A leader who is respected will be able to get their team to do the hard work that is needed far better than a leader who is feared but not respected.

Today we will be looking at how to be respected as a leader without having to use fear to lead.

Hour 1: Classroom Instruction

Ask your campers to list skills they respect in leaders. After you get a few answers, explain the following ways leaders earn respect.

Be Willing to Do the Work Your Staff Does

If you as a leader are not willing to show that you will also be working hard with them they will not respect you. If you give your team all the hard, dirty jobs and you take the easy jobs, staff will quickly notice and not respect you.

Be on Time

Want to lose the respect of your team members? Be late all the time and do not treat their time with the same respect you demand of your time.

Be Consistent

Your team needs to know that what you say one day will be the same the next day. Now there are times when information changes and that impacts your decisions but communicate that information to your staff. You need to be a consistent leader.

Do Not Scapegoat

> *A ruler should be slow to punish and swift to reward.*
> —Ovid

You may have had a boss who could not accept responsibility for anything and blamed everyone else for problems. Do not be that boss. You as a leader need to be the one who takes responsibility. Nothing will destroy a team faster than if they think the leader will unfairly blame them for something that goes wrong. Nothing will build a team up faster than a leader who takes responsibility even when something is not their fault.

Final Notes

Remember: Respect is earned not granted and not bought. You cannot force people to respect you by fear of what you will do or by your money. You can only earn their respect by your actions.

Questions for Campers

- Which of these tips do you think is most important?
- How do you think you can use these tips to earn respect with your fellow campers?
- Do you have any additional tips?

Hour 2: Games/Activities

During this hour campers should be getting ready for their weekly project. This is also a perfect time to finish any one-on-one evaluations you still need to do.

Hour 3: Free Work Time

During this hour campers should work on their final project and hopefully lead an activity with campers or prepare for the night activity they will lead.

Week 3

To command is to serve, nothing more and nothing less.
—Andre Malraux

As we enter Week 3 we will focus on communication. No matter how you set up your program make sure communication is a big part of it. Being a great communicator is one of the best ways to get ahead in life, and it is a skill that can be learned.

Day 1: Practicing Communication*

In Week 1 we talked about improving communication skills. Today we are going to give the campers more real-life experience with how they can improve their communication skills. Each camper will get a speaking assignment and must present to the other CITs/LITs.

Hour 1: Classroom Instruction

During this hour recap the keys to being a good communicator. Assign your CITs/LITs topics. Use topics, such as how to sweep a cabin, a short history of the camp, or a leader they respect and why.

Use the next two or three days, depending on the size of your group, to let them present to the group.

How to Improve Communication

There are several ways to improve communication skills. Start with these.

Communicate Both in Writing and Verbally

Not everyone learns the same way. Some CITs/LITs are audible learners; others need it in writing. As a leader it is important to not only tell your team something but also clearly put it in writing so they can look it over again in the future.

Whenever possible put important information both in writing and verbally to ensure there is no confusion.

Be Clear and Concise

As a leader one of the best things to do when giving directions and instruction is to be clear and concise. We can confuse people by dragging out conversations instead of getting to the point. When you are making an announcement or giving instructions be direct and brief.

When conversations go long, send a follow-up email breaking down the key points.

Make Eye Contact

Whenever you are talking in front of a group of people or even one on one, making eye contact is crucial. It builds credibility and keeps people focused on what you are saying.

If you are in a group, make eye contact for short moments with as many people as possible.

Respect Your Audience

Sometimes it can be easy to talk down to an audience and make them feel that you are being rude to them. Know your audience. Be respectful of the people you are talking with.

Double Check

Do your best to communicate accurate information. Mistakes happen but repeatedly telling your staff incorrect information is a quick way to lose trust. Double check the information you communicate especially when it is in writing.

Hour 2: Practice

Give campers this hour to prepare their presentations for the following days.

Hour 3: Group Work & Project Time

Consider assigning the campers a new weekly project with new group leaders. They can also work on the big project.

Day 2: Presentations

Today is the first day of camper presentations. The hope is to help them become comfortable with public speaking. Do not let campers back out. Many will argue they are too scared. Work with them to overcome their fears because leaders need to speak to groups often.

Hour 1: Presentations

Take your time and do not rush the campers even if it means you need to use extra time. Make sure everyone claps and is supportive to each camper. Set the expectation and maybe even present first to give them an example.

Remember: Public speaking is a learned skill.

Hour 2: Games/Activities

Consider a bigger fun game for your campers like Egg Drop or Scavenger Hunt.

Hour 3: Group Work & Project Time

Continue to work on a group project and take time to ask campers how they are using the skills they are learning on their projects.

Day 3: Presentations: Part 2

Finish presentations and, if you need more time, you can go an extra day or use your second hour.

Hour 1: Classroom Instruction

Use this time to finish the presentations and give sandwich-style feedback.

Hour 2: Games/Activities

Use this time to finish the presentation or give your campers an activity that is not only fun but also forces them to think with the skills they have learned. You can use The Jelly Bean game from the activities list to have them use communication skills in a real-world activity.

Hour 3: Free Work Time & Project Time

We are now halfway through your weekly project time and, for many camps, are starting to get close to the big project. Touch base with your campers to see how they are doing on their timelines.

Day 4: Social Media

As a leader you are a public figure. Later, as your leadership grows, your public presence will also grow. It is important that campers start now to be aware of the dangers of social media. Social media can not only destroy your career but also your personal life.

Today we are going to go over a few tips on how to act on social media as a leader.

Hour 1: Classroom Instruction

Ask your campers if they know anyone who has posted something on social media that later came back to haunt them.

Today everyone needs to be careful on social media like Facebook, Twitter, and Instagram but leaders need to be even more careful. Some people will spend hours if not days digging through social media to find a mistake you made so they can publicly embarrass you. Sometimes it is just for fun and sometimes it is to get your job or get even with you.

As you become a leader you become a public figure first with the team members you work with and then with the people you work for. It is important to be careful all the time with social media.

How to Protect Yourself on Social Media

There are many ways to protect yourself on social media.

Privatize Yourself

Everyone should set their personal social media accounts to private so only people you approve can see your content. This does not mean you can post anything you want, but it is a good way to help protect yourself on social media. Keep in mind not to post anything you do not want the whole world to see.

Only Accept People You Know to Your Personal Social Media

Be *very* selective in who you add to your personal social media accounts. Be careful of random people asking to be friends. You never know what their goals are.

Create a Public Social Media Account

Create a public social media account to promote yourself but with only the content you want out there. Having a public-only Instagram and keeping the one for your family members private is a way to be safe but still use social media.

Remember: Some relationships end and not always positively, so carefully consider what you send to anyone.

Delete Older Posts

Did you know there are free services that will delete any tweet that is older than six months, for example? This helps you not worry that some random comment from when you were younger will come back and haunt you in your twenties and thirties as you start a company, climb the corporate ladder, or serve your community.

Use Strong Passwords & Two-Factor Authentication

You may have heard that you should never use the same password you do with your bank on other sites. The same is true with social media. Hackers will access usernames and passwords from smaller sites to get into larger sites.

Most social media accounts will allow you to use two-factor authentication. This means before you can login they will text you a code to make sure it is really you. It may seem like a pain today, but it could save your career someday.

Final Thoughts

Talk about how increasingly leaders and athletes are having posts from ten-plus years ago leaked on social media. You may not think it can happen to you, but people are spending days and more to hunt through social media posts to destroy someone they do not like or agree with.

Read a few examples you found in the news to your campers to enforce this point.

Hour 2: Games/Activities

If you want to help your campers lock down their social media accounts and your camp allows them access to phones or computers to do that it may be a good use of their time. If not, run an activity to teach them communication to build off this week's speaking assignments. A game like Leading the Blind that forces campers to instruct blindfolded campers through a maze as found in your suggested activities section is a great idea. Make sure to read the entire game description to play it safely.

Hour 3: Free Work & Projects

With this week's projects coming due tomorrow make sure to touch base with each group to ensure that the projects are on track. Help without doing.

Day 5: Self-Care

We are now three weeks into the CIT/LIT program. This is the point where many campers will start to show signs of the hard work they have been putting into the program. Hopefully, you have been able to give them an area to unwind in after evening programming and worked in days off for them. Today we are going to talk about how they can keep themselves fresh so they can continue working at the highest levels possible.

Hopefully, these tips will help you avoid burn out. When you burn out, it can cause you to make bad decisions and affect your physical health.

Hour 1: Classroom Instruction

Ask your campers, "Have you ever had a time that you felt rundown?" "Have you ever been burnt out?" Burn out is avoidable if you take care of yourself. Proper self-care can make you a far happier person and help you be a better worker along with a better leader.

Tips to Being a Better Leader

These tips may seem obvious, but if you start practicing them now, they will help you as a leader and in your private life too.

Get Sleep

One of the first things to go when things get crazy is sleep, but it should be one of the last things you let slip. When you fail to sleep you are setting yourself up for long-term burn out. This cannot end in anything but lower quality work.

Winston Churchill, one of the greatest leaders of the Twentieth Century, led Britain through the Second World War. He would regularly take afternoon naps. Sometimes we feel that we need to be seen 24/7, but the truth is a little sleep can go a long way.

Eat Better

It is easier than ever to eat well. With food delivery services and premade meals ready to be put in the oven, it has never been easier to eat healthy food.

Drink plenty of water and skip bad snacks. Skipping that coffee, energy drink, or soda and replacing it with water can help you have better mental health.

Find What Makes You Relax

Everyone is different at what makes them relax. For me a round of golf or thirty minutes playing video games can completely relax me. Ask yourself what relaxes you and make sure you do it every week.

Do not be afraid to go for a walk in the middle of the day. If a fifteen-minute walk helps you, the benefits will outweigh any lost time.

Ask your campers what relaxes them. Kick around some ideas and point out how we are all different when it comes to what helps us relax.

Avoid the Temptation of Using Substances

This is a serious topic that most people avoid, but over the last twenty years alcohol-related deaths have doubled. What is especially scary is that the number of women dying from alcohol-related causes is skyrocketing.

It may be shocking to find out that many of the people who die from substance abuse are highly educated professionals (aka leaders). The stress of the job plus the thought that this cannot happen to me can be a huge downfall. Drinking is highest among educated and upper-income Americans overall and we need to talk to campers now about it and other substances that could hurt them.

Make sure to tread lightly but do not shy away from this difficult but important topic.

Take time to talk to your campers about the dangers of becoming reliant on chemicals to get you through your day and how that can in the long run cause personal pain. Challenge them to not assume it cannot happen to them because statistically the campers you are working with are some of the most at danger of abusing alcohol and other drugs.

Take a Break

I admit I am bad at taking a break. I worked for almost six straight years without taking a single day off as I grew my company. In the end, it just burnt me out and hurt my ability to keep growing my company. Remind yourself to stop and take a break. Go on that vacation and find time for that dinner out with family and friends. It will pay off far more than you know.

Questions for Campers

- Which one of these tactics to avoid burn out do you think you are worse at?
- Which one do you think is most important to you?

- When is the last time you felt burnt out? What caused it? Looking back could you have avoided burning out?

Hour 2: Games/Activities

Consider having an activity here that forces them to think as a group. The What If or the Point of View games would fit well here.

Feel free to let campers use this time to prepare for their weekly activity that is happening today.

Hour 3: Projects & Free Work Time

During this time campers should be leading their weekly projects or preparing for their project later in the day.

Week 4

The best executive is the one who has sense enough to pick good men to do what he wants done, and self-restraint enough to keep from meddling with them while they do it.
—Theodore Roosevelt

As we move into Week 4, we are going to get deeper into select topics. Our goal is to give campers information that will not only help them be great camp counselors someday but also help them in their lives outside of camp. Always keep that goal in mind as you work through this program.

Day 1: Seeing What & Where You Are Leading

*You don't lead by pointing and telling people some place to go.
You lead by going to that place and making a case.*
—Ken Kesey

Once I had an opportunity to watch some Army majors talk about a planned troop exercise. They pointed to an area on a map that looked like a great place to set up a company of soldiers. Everyone—except for one major—quickly agreed that it would be perfect. He asked if anyone had been there or investigated what kind of land it was. He already knew it was swampland because he had traveled that area, but you would never know it was swampland just by looking at the map.

A good leader needs to know exactly where he is sending his team and with what they will be working. Without it this group of Army majors would have sent soldiers into a swamp.

Today we will be working with campers on the importance of seeing where they are leading people and knowing exactly what they will be working with before sending them. It is on you as a leader to set your team up for success.

Hour 1: Classroom Instruction

Ask your campers how effective a leader can be if they have never seen what or who they are leading. Push them to think about how a leader can lead people and things that they have never seen.

Today, it is likely you will work with people and in places you have never been to or met face to face, but that does not mean you cannot learn about them and what they are doing.

It is important to learn as much about where you are leading as possible from online sources and accounts of people who have been there. Whenever possible onsite is the best way to learn.

Teaching hands on is best. Consider using an activity like Leading the Blind where campers talk blindfolded team members through a maze. Make sure to read the instructions on how to do this safely.

Hour 2: Games/Activities

If you did not do it during classroom time, consider using an activity like Leading the Blind where campers talk blindfolded team members through a maze. Make sure to read the instructions on how to do this safely.

Hour 3: Project & Free Work Time

If you have time for a new weekly project, divide your campers into new groups and assign new leaders.

Move the big project forward. At this point planning should be far enough along that if they are leading a big all-camp activity the campers should hold meetings with the owners/directors to present their plans and get feedback. This is a great opportunity to help campers learn about meetings and making presentations by doing.

Day 2: Dealing with Burn Out

We talked about how to avoid burn out in our self-care section but what happens when you hit burn out? How can you recover from burn out and get back to work?

Today we are going to focus on the signs of burn out and tips on overcoming it.

Hour 1: Classroom Instruction

We have all experienced burn out at some point, and we all respond to it differently. As we go through these signs of burn out and ways to get over it, remember not all of them may apply to you. Listen to your body.

Burn out can have real physical side effects including heart disease and diabetes. Consider directly dealing with burn out not just for your mental health but also your physical health.

Warning Signs of Burn Out

The following are some warning signs of burn out.

- Lack of Enjoyment in Your Work
- Cynical/Critical Look at Work
- Lack of Energy & Productivity
- Struggling to Concentrate
- Difficulty Sleeping
- Physical Complications

Tips to Avoid Burn Out

There are many ways to avoid burn out. Here are a few.

Ask for Help

Sometimes as leaders we take on more work than we should, and this leads us to overwork and burn out. When you start to experience burn out, one of the best ways to stop it is to delegate or assign work you do not need to perform yourself early on.

Do your best to be aware of how much work you can handle and understand that can change from time to time. Personal life and work issues may mean you need to focus on fewer things and delegate more.

Exercise

As leaders, we often stop focusing on our physical health but being physical, whether by going to the gym or taking a walk, is one of the best ways to reduce stress and burn out. Build exercise into your schedule. Even mild activity can dramatically lower stress and burn out.

Get Sleep

One of the main causes of burn out is not getting enough sleep. Make sure to get regular sleep to accommodate your work and physical activity levels.

Relax

Sometimes burn out comes from stress, and no reduction in activity can help if you do not address your stress level. Each of us have different stress levels, so we must find ways to handle it individually. Consider reducing your stress by talking about it or finding a hobby that helps you release it.

If your stress level is extremely high and stays high no matter what you do, consider talking to a professional.

Take a Break

Taking a break seems easy, but many leaders skip it. Sometimes you just need to take a long weekend or a week off to reset your mind and body. Do not be afraid to take that vacation you want. It may make you an even better worker helping you get more done than if you had just kept working overtime.

Questions for Campers

- Which one of these warning signs have you experienced?

- Have you seen or used any of the tips?
- What would you add to this list?

Hour 2: Games/Activities

As we are now four weeks in, consider giving your campers some extra time off to relax and recharge.

Hour 3: Project Time/Free Work

Touch base with your project leaders. Ask them to present to you an update on what they are doing. Push them to step up their game this week.

Day 3: The Dangers of Scapegoating

A ruler should be slow to punish and swift to reward.
—Ovid

Someone made a mistake. You did not make the mistake, but the person who did is on your team. It is easy to point a finger at that person and blame them to save yourself. Yet having a scapegoat is one of the worst things you can do because it will destroy all faith in you as a leader.

One of the best ways to earn respect as a leader is when something goes wrong you accept responsibility for it.

Today we are going to look at why you need to accept responsibility as a leader for what is happening around you even when it is not your fault.

The greatest danger comes from scapegoating someone who did nothing wrong. This will quickly destroy any credibility and trust you had with your team.

Hour 1: Classroom Instruction

Ask your campers if they have ever seen someone blame others to protect themselves when things went wrong. Get them to talk about how that made them feel about the person who blamed others.

Follow up by asking if they have ever seen someone take responsibility for something that went wrong when they could have blamed someone who really did deserve it. Ask them how that made them feel about that person.

During World War II, Winston Churchill was well known for not blaming the people who worked closely with him. When things would go wrong—even if the other person advocated for it or oversaw it—Churchill would take responsibility. This meant his close group of staff were extremely loyal to him. This loyalty later protected him when people tried to force him out.

Consider talking about experiences you had in your life when people did scapegoat someone or took responsibility when they did not need to.

Ways to Take Responsibility

The following three ways to take responsibility are just the beginning. There are other ways to show you take responsibility as well. Do your own research to find other ways that may better suit you.

Publicly Take Responsibility

Sometimes as a leader you need to stand up and make it clear in writing or verbally that you take responsibility for what is happening. Consider publicly and even maybe in writing taking responsibility to show you are in charge.

Show You Take Responsibility

When something goes wrong the best way to take responsibility is to clearly lay out a plan, so it does not happen again. Consider posting several ways you plan to prevent what happened from happening again so everyone can see your plan.

Move Forward

As a leader sometimes you must get things moving again. Spend the time needed on a mistake or issue and move forward. Avoid the temptation to stop moving forward when something goes wrong.

Questions for Campers

- What is the hardest part of taking responsibility?

- Why do you think most people refuse to take responsibility?
- Do you struggle with taking responsibility?

Hour 2: Games/Activities

Consider using games that force your campers to think. For example, The Tower game, which is a physical mind game, or This or That?

Hour 3: Projects & Free Work

We are halfway through the weekly project and for many halfway through the big final project. Have your campers make a presentation to you on what they are planning to do. Help them become more comfortable speaking in front of others.

Day 4: The Power of Brainstorming & Diversity

One of the most powerful tools any leader can have is a diverse team of people they respect. However, if you want to get the full benefit of a diverse group of people giving you advice they need to feel they can speak their minds even when you may not like what they have to say.

Having a diverse group of people around you will not help you if they are not willing to speak up.

Today we are going to focus on how to brainstorm with your team to get fresh new ideas and make sure your team is willing to speak up.

Hour 1: Classroom Instruction

Push home the idea that diversity only truly helps a leader if they are willing to consider other people's views. To do this, you need to create an environment or culture where brainstorming is encouraged.

Ways to Encourage Brainstorming

The following are a few ways to encourage brainstorming.

Be Clear & Open

If you want people to give you their honest opinion you need to be honest with them about wanting it. Sometimes all it takes is saying, "What do you think of this idea?" or "What would you do?" to get your team to start talking.

Ask and make it clear you want their feedback, and you may be surprised at how many people will open up.

Give Them Time to Think

Rarely do we get our best ideas on the spot or in an hour-long meeting. People need time to think and develop good ideas. Consider sending over the project or issue you want to talk out a day—or even a few hours—before a meeting. Give them time to come up with ideas at the meeting. This can dramatically improve the feedback you get.

Write It All Down

Put it all down so everyone can see the ideas being passed around. This could be done on a big white board or in an email following the meeting. Sometimes we forget something that was said, and you never know if that was the key piece of information that is needed.

Do not just talk. Put it all down in writing so no one misses out on a great idea.

Give Positive Feedback Even When You Do Not Like the Idea

Not every idea is a great idea but do not beat anyone up over it. Consider giving some positive feedback as you point out the issue. Something like "That's a great idea, but I am concerned about xyz" or "Love the thought but worried we won't be able to make it work."

These positive statements can help them think of a way to overcome the issues in their idea or maybe show you an idea you did not think about. If you turn them down in a negative way, they may not be willing to point out something you may have missed.

Give positive feedback even when you do not like the idea. You never know, they may surprise you and that is the point of brainstorming.

Never Give Your Views Too Early

One of the ways a leader can kill brainstorming is to make their point of view known right at the start. Hold on to your ideas or you could just fall into groupthink. Let staff present their ideas before you present your ideas.

Questions for Campers

- Which of these ideas do you think is most important?
- How would you like your boss to let you know your opinion is valuable?
- Have you ever had to take responsibility when something went wrong? What happened?

Final Thoughts

Let your campers know that tomorrow you will be brainstorming a topic. Give them something that needs to be done like a new theme week at camp—something never done before—or have them come up with ideas to improve their school and life outside of camp.

Hour 2: Free Work

Have your campers work on their ideas to present on the assigned topic for tomorrow.

Hour 3: Free Time/Project Time

Tomorrow is the big day for the weekly project. Consider having them present their work for their big program.

Day 5: Brainstorming

Today in class we are going to spend an hour brainstorming. Give campers the real feel of what it is like in a meeting to get ideas out and come up with a decision. At the end of the meeting the campers must all pick one or two ideas to move forward with based on the arguments made today.

Hour 1: Brainstorming

Review the topic we are discussing. Make sure to use all the tips we talked about yesterday. Have fun and do your best to get the conversation moving and have each camper present their idea.

Hour 2: Free Work/Project Time

Today is the day for the weekly project so use this time to set up and prepare.

Hour 3: Projects

Have your campers lead their projects now or in the evening depending on what they are doing.

Week 5

Men make history and not the other way around. In periods where there is no leadership,
society stands still. Progress occurs when courageous, skillful leaders seize the
opportunity to change things for the better.
—Harry S. Truman

This week we are going to focus on communication again. This may seem like overkill, but many people struggle with effective communication. Take the time to give your campers as many chances as possible to improve their communication skills.

Day 1: Practicing Communication Again*

In Weeks 1 and 3 we talked about improving communication skills and had campers practice public speaking. Today we are going to help the campers get more real-life experience by having them practice again.

Each camper will get a speaking assignment and must present to the other CITs/LITs. This time they will need a visual aid they can make in Power Point or on poster board.

Give them a target time of ten minutes for their talk.

Hour 1: Classroom Instruction

During this hour recap the keys to being a good communicator. Also assign topics. Use topics like how to sweep a cabin, a short history of the camp, or a leader they respect and why.

Use the next two or three days for presentations.

How to Improve Communication

The following tips help you improve communication skills.

Communicate Both in Writing and Verbally

Not everyone learns the same way. Some people are audible learners; others need it in writing. As a leader it is important to not only tell your team something but also clearly put it in writing so they can look it over again in the future.

Whenever possible put important information in writing and announce it verbally to make sure there is no confusion.

Be Clear and Concise

As a leader one of the best things to do when giving direction and instruction is to be direct and brief. Often we can confuse people by dragging out conversations instead of getting to the point. When you are making an announcement or giving instructions be clear and concise.

When conversations go long, send a follow-up email breaking down the key points.

Make Eye Contact

Whenever you are talking in front of a group of people, or even one on one, making eye contact is crucial. It builds credibility and keeps people focused on what you are saying.

If you are in a group, make eye contact for short moments with as many people as possible.

Respect Your Audience

It can be easy to talk down to an audience and make them feel that you are being rude to them. Research your audience beforehand. Do your best to be respectful of the people you are talking with.

Double Check

Give accurate information. Mistakes happen but repeatedly telling your staff incorrect information is a quick way to lose trust. Double check everything you communicate especially when it is in writing.

Hour 2: Practice

Give campers this hour to prepare their presentations.

Hour 3: Group Work & Project Time

During this hour consider assigning the campers a new weekly project with new group leaders. Also use it as time for the big project.

Day 2: Presentations

Today is the first day of presentations. The hope is to help them become comfortable speaking in front of others. Do not let campers back out. Many will argue they are too scared. Work with them to overcome their fears to help them become better leaders.

Hour 1: Presentations

Take your time and do not rush the campers even if it means you need to use extra time. Make sure everyone claps and is supportive of each other. Set the expectations and maybe even present first to give them an example.

Remember: Public speaking is a learned skill.

Hour 2: Games/Activities

Consider a bigger fun game for your campers like Egg Drop or Scavenger Hunt.

Hour 3: Group Work & Project Time

Continue to work on the group project and ask campers how they are using the skills they are learning to work on their projects.

Day 3: Presentations: Part 2

Finish presentations and, if you need more time, you can go an extra day or use your second hour.

Hour 1: Classroom Instruction

Use this time to continue the presentations and give feedback.

Hour 2: Games/Activities

Finish the presentations or give your campers an activity that is not only fun but also forces them to think with the skills they have learned.

Hour 3: Free Work Time & Project Time

Help your campers with their projects and keep pushing them to finish strong.

Day 4: Setting Realistic Goals

Since the start of this project, we have been setting daily and weekly goals. Now talk about big picture goals: The goals that build companies and the goals that we build our lives around. You need good realistic goals.

A bad goal can destroy your company and your life. Today we are going to look at how to set smart goals that will help you grow.

Hour 1: Classroom Instruction

Goals are a great thing if they are realistic. That does not mean you cannot dream big. It means the goals need to be reasonable and achievable. When you let an unrealistic goal control you, you are setting yourself up for failure from the start. When that happens, you waste time and, more importantly, mental energy on an unrealistic goal.

Ask your campers to give their opinions on what makes a goal unachievable. Push them to think about what makes a realistic goal.

Tips to Making Realistic Goals

The following are tips on making realistic goals.

Set Specific & Measurable Goals

A goal is not a real goal unless you can clearly define what it is and measure it. Saying I want to be famous someday is not a goal you can measure. Saying I want 100,000 followers on social media is a measurable goal that is clearly defined.

Relevant & Realistic Goals

Goals are great but if your goal is to make sure you get coffee in the morning that is not a relevant goal. Make goals that are related to what you are doing or plan to do. Do not get caught up in small goals that do not help you achieve your long-term goals.

Set a Timeline

A goal is only a goal if there is some timeline attached to it. Wanting 100,000 followers on social media can be something you always work for if you do not have a set timeline for it. With a timeline, you will find it becomes something you have to work for instead of something you just hope happens.

Goals need a date and time you want to achieve them by, or they are just a dream.

Homework

Tell your campers to write two goals that are specific, measurable, realistic, and have a timeline to complete them in before the end of camp. They will need to present their goals during the first hour tomorrow. (One more way to get them comfortable speaking in front of others.) You also want them to set one goal to be completed when they get back home.

Questions for Campers

- What goals do you have?
- Do you think they are realistic?
- How could you make them realistic?

Hour 2: Activities/Free Work

Consider letting your campers use this time to set their goals and work on their presentation. With so much happening as the projects come to an end additional work outside of class time is recommended.

Hour 3: Free Work/Project Time

Tomorrow is the final day for this week's project, and we are coming close to an end. Work with your campers to complete the tasks assigned in the time allotted.

Day 5: Goal Presentations

Today serves two purposes: First, to give campers one more opportunity to speak in front of people to help them become more confident in their speaking abilities; and second, to help them learn to make goals that they can clearly communicate.

Hours 1 & 2: Presentations

During your goal presentations we want the campers to work on their goals and be able to answer questions. You want campers to stand up and present their three goals to the group. At the end of each camper's presentation, ask them some questions and have the group ask them questions about their goals. Use this method to help them defend their goals each day.

Hour 3: Free Work/Project Time

During this time campers should be engaging in their final projects for the week.

Week 6

The art of leadership is saying no, not saying yes. It is very easy to say yes.
—Tony Blair

This week we have a few goals. First, to touch base with all campers as they work on their projects through their evaluations. Our goal is to teach them to evaluate themselves and how to evaluate others. Also, we hope to give them a resume they can take home and use after they leave camp. So many people have great skills, but they lack the ability to communicate those skills to possible employers. Hopefully, we can help them with this important life skill.

Day 1: Evaluations*

Today we give campers their second official evaluations. Taking an honest look at yourself is hard but having others examine you can be even harder. What may surprise people is how difficult it is to give a good, honest evaluation of your team members.

Make sure that we are giving them goals to work on. We are now over halfway through the CIT/LIT program.

Hour 1: Classroom Instruction

In this section we will look at evaluations and the three main goals that every leader must evaluate team members on. Today, we will look at them and give tips on how do an evaluation with a team member.

Before you start, it is important to do your research. Learn what should be happening with the work. Make sure you make notes and have what you want to say clear before you meet with them. Nothing will lose the respect of your team members like not having any idea what they do.

Also, when you give feedback take time to listen to your staff and give them an opportunity to respond. You may learn something important. Plus, they will respect you for taking the time to listen.

Give your campers a goal you want them to work on over the next few weeks of the training. Make this something that just you and they know about.

Make sure to compliment them more than you make suggestions for areas to improve. This helps campers feel good about the evaluation and more willing to work on being better.

Quality of Work and Taking Ownership

We all understand the quality of work is someone doing a good job, but what about initiative? Do you as a leader need to walk them step by step through everything or do they take the reins to deal with any issues that come up in their area?

Talk with your staff about areas to improve and, more importantly, areas they are excelling at.

Be on Time & on Budget

Being on time has many meanings such as showing up to work on time. Yet one of the most important tasks for an employee is to meet deadlines. If one person is always late it can slow down the team. Take this time to look at how they are doing with their timelines. Also discuss honest and reachable budgetary goals.

Consider using the campers project budget as an example of budget work.

Working as a Team

We all have that time where we just wish we could do a project by ourselves, but the truth is that is not always possible. You must work with others as a team, and how you do that is important. Talk with your staff about how they are a good member of the team, how they are working with other members, and handling any issues within the team.

Final Notes

I highly suggest always starting with some positive feedback and moving to an area to improve on. Wrap up with one last positive area.

End by telling your campers you will be meeting with each of them to talk about their progress and see how you can help them move forward.

Hour 2: One-on-One Evaluations

Start the one-on-one evaluations. Make sure to do them in a public area where others can see you. The other campers can work on their projects during this time.

Hour 3: Project Time

Consider assigning the campers a new weekly project with new group leaders. Also use it as time for the big project.

Day 2: Evaluations & Community Service Projects

Finish the one-on-one evaluations and start a community service project. This time, your campers will be responsible for deciding what they will do and where.

Hour 1: Classroom Instruction

Inform your campers that they will be responsible for picking an area nonprofit they want to volunteer with as a massive group. They must decide what the nonprofit is, call them, and schedule a few hours to work. I set this time in this example as Friday morning, but please adjust as needed.

The campers will need to set goals and find a way to implement them as a group. Offer minimal help. Let them do this work.

The campers must first create a short presentation for you about where they want to go and how they plan to help. What will be needed? Have them do this and get your approval before they call.

Once they make the call and get the approval have them present the results of the call to you in a meeting format.

If taking them offsite is not possible, consider having them decide on a project around the camp and talk with the camp director to set it up.

Hour 2: Evaluations & Free Work

Complete any evaluations and continue to work on the community service project.

Hour 3: Free Work & Project Time

Use this time for your community service project.

Day 3: Building Your Resume

A resume is your first and sometimes only opportunity to make an impression, but what if you do not have a lot of experience and you want the job? The good news is high schoolers can start now to build their resume to get the job and career they want.

Today we offer the campers some practical tips on building and writing a resume.

Hour 1: Classroom Instruction

We all want something in life and if it is work related the number one way to get it is by having a good resume. Your resume is your first impression, and your social media is your second. So, remember to put effort into making them look nice.

We are also going to make a resume in Microsoft Word that you can email to yourself. Having a resume ready means when an interesting opportunity comes along you can quickly and easily update your current resume and send it over.

First, before we talk about the resume we need to discuss what you can put on it. High schoolers think they have nothing to put on a resume but often they do. The truth is you likely have a lot of information to include.

Non-Work-Related Activities

The following are some non-work-related activities that high schoolers should consider putting on their resume:

- Extracurricular activities (like this CIT/LIT program)
- Sports or clubs
- Part-time jobs, including babysitting and yard work
- GPA (if it is good)
- Skills or accomplishments
- College-level classes
- Service work

Information That Should Be on Every Resume

The following information should be on your resume:

- Basic information including name and how to contact you. Make sure to include both an email and a phone number.
- Your current education level
- Non-work-related experience
- If you speak any other languages
- Awards or honors

Consider putting a sample resume up for them to use as a template.

Homework

Campers should create a resume on a computer if possible. If not, have them write everything down and they can take it home and type it up later.

To help your campers, grab one of the free resume templates that come with Microsoft Word. If your campers do not have Word, consider using a free word editing program like Google Docs or Open Office.

Work with your campers to create a resume they can use after this program ends. Have them turn it in to you to review and add feedback.

Hour 2: Resume Work

Work with your campers on creating a resume. After they turn them in, make some notes for improvements and send them back to the campers.

Hour 3: Project Time & Community Service

Continue working with them on their projects and setting up community service.

Day 4: Interviewing Tips & Practice

Now that we created resumes, today we are going to be talking about tips for interviewing. Next week campers will be doing one-on-one interviews with you for a job as an assistant director of the camp.

Hour 1: Classroom Instruction

So, you got the interview based on your resume. Now you need to impress them with who you are.

In life you will be interviewed in many situations, not just for work. From a date to applying to volunteer to finding housing you may be interviewed at any time. Even as a business owner a sales meeting with a new client is an interview.

Interview Tips

The following are a few tips for successful interviews.

Dress for the Job

If you want the job you need to dress appropriately. That does not mean a three-piece business suit for every interview. Some companies are more formal than others. Do a little research online to learn about the culture.

Remember: It is better to be slightly overdressed than underdressed even in today's more relaxed work world.

Being Early Is on Time

Do not be late! Also do not be on time. You want to be a few minutes early so you are ready when they are ready for you. The worst thing possible is to show up on time but find you need to go through security before your interview making you late to meet with the interviewer. Make sure you show up a little early, but not too early either.

Do Your Research

You should know something about the company you are interviewing with. Reading their about us section on their website is a start but also look at their social media and even Wikipedia to learn more about them.

Showing you took the time to learn about them will help you stand out.

Be Polite & Respectful

Sometimes things go wrong during an interview on both sides. You may show up and the company may have mistakenly double booked two interviews at once. Or the person running the interview may have an emergency. You need to respond politely and respectfully in every situation.

Was this double booking a mistake or an attempt to see how you will respond? Keep that in mind.

Pay Attention

One of the worst things you can do during an interview is not pay attention to the interviewer. Do your best to maintain eye contact and smile when appropriate. Smiling with eye contact makes you look strong and confident in your abilities. Get a business card, too, so you can follow up later.

Say Thank You & Follow Up

After the interview is over make sure to thank them for the interview and their time. Send a follow-up email later that day or the next day thanking them for the opportunity to interview and highlight why you would be a good fit possibly in relation to some new information you learned during the interview.

Interview Questions

Campers should be prepared to answer the following questions in an interview.

- Why do you want this job?
- What are your strengths?
- What are your weaknesses?
- What do you do for fun?
- What do you enjoy about school?
- What makes someone a good teacher?

Preparing for Next Week

Next week we will be doing one-on-one interviews with each camper. The campers will be applying to be the assistant camp director at your camp. Do not rush these interviews and give each camper fifteen to twenty minutes.

Hours 2–3: Free Work

During this time let your campers work on their projects including volunteering. Make any changes needed to their resumes and prepare for their community service project tomorrow.

Day 5: Community Service

Today was kept clear so your campers could complete their community service project. They can also use the day to complete their weekly project.

After the community service project is finished talk about how they did and what they thought about being one hundred percent responsible for that project.

Week 7

The very essence of leadership is that you have to have a vision. It's got to be a vision you articulate clearly and forcefully on every occasion. You can't blow an uncertain trumpet.
—Reverend Theodore Hesburgh

We are almost done with the program. Now we are moving a lot more into the practical side of putting what we learned into practice. Over the next few weeks, we have classroom work, but we are going to continue to focus on giving them skills they need in life and putting what we learned to use.

Days 1–3: Interviews*

Start three days of one-on-one interviews. The exact time you need will vary depending on how many campers you have. Give a quick recap of interview tips and do your best to make this a fun, relaxing experience.

When campers are not being interviewed have them work on their group projects. Campers should be at the final stages of preparation. Encourage them to practice their presentations.

If you need extra time, consider having them shadow leaders around camp for the day. Find a camp leader who will be willing to not only have youth follow them but also explain what they do and why they do it.

Day 4: Treating Others with Respect

*The challenge of leadership is to be strong, but not rude; be kind, but not weak; be bold,
but not bully; be thoughtful, but not lazy; be humble, but not timid; be proud, but not arrogant;
have humor, but without folly.*
—Jim Rohn

Treating others with respect seems like an easy thing to do, but it is a little harder than you would think. Today we will look at how you as a leader can treat those around you with respect.

Hour 1: Classroom Instruction

Talk with your staff about how people above them have treated them with respect. This could be teachers, bosses, or youth group leaders. How did it make them feel when they were treated with respect? How about times superiors failed to treat them with respect? How did that make them feel?

Ways to Treat Others with Respect

The following are a few ways to treat others with respect.

Be Polite & Kind When Mistakes Are Made

Being polite and kind is easy when you are happy with your employees but what about when they make a mistake. That is the time you need to be kind and polite even when you must correct them.

Control Your Mouth

It is easy to feel like you can talk about other employees when they are not around. As a leader you can *never* do this. Even if that employee does not find out, the staff you talk to will always wonder what you say about them.

As a leader, avoid swearing, name calling, disparaging, or mocking your team members. This is a quick way to lose their respect.

Include Your Team Members

When you leave team members in the dark you are telling them they are not important enough to be informed. Whenever possible keep your team informed on what is happening around them.

Nothing is worse than finding out others knew what was happening, but you did not. Keeping your team aware of what is happening is also a way to keep them engaged in your organization's success.

Listen to Others

Avoid the temptation to say you know everything. Make sure your team knows you are willing to listen to them. Nothing says I do not respect you like turning down an idea or an offer without hearing it. Listen to your team members.

Encourage Your Team Members

Encourage others. Take a moment to let them know you are thinking of them and appreciate them.

Questions for Campers

- Which one of these ways to show respect do you most enjoy receiving?
- Have you ever been rude to someone when you did not mean to? How did it happen?
- Would you add anything to the list?

Hour 2: Activities/Free Work

Projects are due tomorrow. Feel free to use this time to complete the projects or do an activity.

Hour 3: Project Time & Community Service

Continue working with them on their projects and on setting up the community service project.

Day 5: Project Day

If you have not done so by now you need to have your campers present their final project for approval. With only two weeks left you need them working on the final project after you approve it.

This day can be adjusted as you see fit to fall when you need it to.

For the rest of the day have the campers work on finishing and running their weekly projects.

Week 8

A good general not only sees the way to victory; he also knows when victory is impossible.
—Polybius

With only a few more weeks left we are going to touch on some important topics that are best learned after having covered some of the earlier topics. Topics like being a better listener are more useful after learning how to be a better communicator.

Day 1: How to Be a Better Listener*

Being a good listener is not something most people are naturally good at, butit is something that can be learned. Today we are going to work with the campers on ways they can become better listeners.

Hour 1: Classroom Instruction

Today we are going to be going over tips on how to become a better listener.

Wait Until They Stop Talking

This one seems simple, but you need to wait until someone has completely stopped talking or you risk missing out on a key point they are trying to communicate. Waiting also shows respect for the person talking.

Ask Questions

Do your best to ask follow-up questions. This makes the person talking feel like you paid attention to them. Make the questions meaningful or do not ask them.

Allow Them to Set the Agenda

Sometimes when a meeting is called you need to let others say what they feel is important. If you try to focus just on what you want to hear you are limiting their ability to bring up something important to them.

Clear Your Mind

We all do it—we zone out when someone talks. This is dangerous. It is rude. People notice. You will also miss important information.

Maintain Eye Contact & Focus on the Speaker

Put away distractions so you can focus on the speaker. Maintaining eye contact shows that you are interested in the speaker and what they have to say.

Questions for Campers

- Which one of these habits do you excel at?
- Which one is a challenge?
- Is there one you want to work on?

Days 2–4: Camp Internships

In the past we talked about having your campers watch camp leaders at work. Now think about having them do internships such as running a day, an activity, or acting as the assistant director or office manager.

The goal is to not have them just watch but to also have them work with the leaders doing part of their job for a few days. Make a big deal about this, and have your campers apply and interview for the internship they want at camp.

Work with the staff who the campers will be working with to guide them in helping the campers learn by doing.

If you cannot do three days of internships do a day or two. One of the best ways we can teach campers to be leaders is giving them opportunities to do just that.

Have your campers work on their projects. No new weekly projects should be assigned unless your program is short and you need to do both.

Day 5: Internship Recap

Spend the day talking with your campers about what they learned during their internship. Have each camper meet with the person they interned with for a one-on-one evaluation.

Use the remaining free time for the final project.

Week 9

A leader takes people where they want to go. A great leader takes people where
they don't necessarily want to go but ought to be.
—Rosalynn Carter

This week our goal is to get the campers to think like a leader and put what they have learned to good use. If your program is shorter than ten weeks, find a day to give them example problems to think about and work on.

What If Week

Use this classroom instruction time to give campers scenarios around camp to work on. We want to get their brains moving as much as possible. Consider having them each come up with a report on the scenario you give them.

Days 1–3: What If Activities

Try to find examples of problems that happened around camp from the previous year. Ask your campers to work on how they would have responded. Have them list tools that they learned this year that would help them.

You can do this in the first hour by breaking campers up to work on a problem to present a plan of action. In the second hour have them present their solution to the problem. This gives campers one more opportunity to practice public speaking but this time as a group.

Have an active listening practice session this week. Have your campers talk to you and then repeat back the key points of what they said. After that flip it around and have them practice picking out the key points you talk about.

If you have yet to do so have your campers practice public speaking.

Days 4–5: Preparing for the Final Push

Next week is the final big push to run the projects that the campers have been working on. This is also the week where you wrap up as the campers prepare to head home. Take these two days to recap anything you feel did not get communicated the first time.

Work with your campers so they are ready for the big project. We want them to be successful, but we don't want to do it all for them. Do your best to balance these two goals.

Week 10: Closing Week

Leaders think and talk about the solutions. Followers think and talk about the problems.
—Brian Tracy

The final week is left open to best fit what you see is needed. If your program is shorter than ten weeks, you may need to cram some classroom instruction into the final week. Use the final week for the campers to run their final big project. This could be leading camp's color war, closing ceremony, etc.

If you have not done so by this point consider having your campers shadow a leader for a day. Find someone who will not only let them see them at work but also explain why they do what they do.

Do your best to have a final party for your campers. They have worked hard. Use the party to bring them together one last time.

Here is a quick rundown of an example week for the final week of camp.

Days 1–2: Final Projects*

Your campers have been working all summer on a big final project. This could be an event like a color war or a closing ceremony for camp. Whatever your campers worked on these are the days they will be dedicated to completing it.

Day 3: Wrapping Up

Take some time to review how the final projects went. Also wrap up any leftover topics before the summer ends.

Day 4: Closing Ceremonies & Party

Separate from the party should be a graduation ceremony. Present them with a certificate that can be used to prove that they completed the CIT/LIT program. Talk to them about taking what they have learned home with them to use as they move forward in life.

Day 5: Goodbye

Right before they leave make sure to give your campers a final talk. Encourage them to take what they have learned and use it outside of camp. Warn them to stay humble and work their way up. Remind them that it takes time to achieve your goals in life. Also, if you have not already, encourage them to come back as staff some day and help them know they have completed something important in life.

He who has great power should use it lightly.
—Seneca

20 Leadership & Teamwork Activities

I learned these leadership and teamwork games at camp. Many of them I learned as a leader and others I participated in as a camper. Feel free to make changes based on what works best for your group and situation. These activities are divided into physical and sedentary or "sit down" activities. Both types of activities get the teens thinking, laughing, and bonding.

Important: Before you pick the activity, remember we are not just having fun here. Make sure to take ten to fifteen minutes at the end of the game to ask follow-up questions to ensure the lessons are also being learned.

Suggestion: If, for any of these activities, you select a youth leader to oversee the other campers, do not critique them in front of the group, especially if you have negative feedback. Pull the leader aside for a one-on-one talk in a public place. This teaches good management skills too (for example, do not criticize or give negative feedback in front of others).

Physical Activities

These physical activities will get teens up, moving, and thinking.

The Tower

The Tower game is a fun way to start team building. It can be used as an opening activity to get a new group of kids working together, and it can also be used to teach a group of leaders.

The Goal

To get the group to communicate and problem solve to build a tower that reaches the goal height.

How to Play

Present Counselors in Training or Leaders in Training (CITs/LITs) with a group of items. They are tasked with building a tower that is a specific height. The staff leader sets a time limit and a goal height. (The height must be reachable but not easily reachable.) The finished tower must stand for one minute without falling and without being held or propped by a CIT/LIT.

There are two ways to play The Tower game. First, there is no assigned leader, and the campers must work together to build the tower. Second, there is an assigned leader who must take all the team suggestions, but who has—in the end—the final say.

Suggestions

Make sure the items you give the campers can reach the desired height but not easily. The items can be all the same, such as cups, or different, such as wood, chairs, and buckets.

A leader should always supervise to make sure no unsafe activities are being done to reach the desired height.

Post-Game Questions

- Other than physically building the tower, what was the most difficult part of this activity?
- If you had to do this again, what changes would you make? Why?
- Was the first idea the one that worked?
- How many ideas did it take to get to the correct answer? Often, we stop at the first good idea without moving on to the second idea or the third idea.

Additional Thoughts

The activity should get the campers thinking about the process they used to build the tower and to teach them to review and learn from their work to help them move forward in becoming great leaders.

The Silent Line

This activity works best in groups of four or more campers. With the Silent Line, campers must line up in a certain order as instructed by the leader, but they cannot talk to each other or write down anything to communicate with other team members. The rules are simple: Youth must use their bodies to communicate. Verbal communication is not allowed. To make the game more difficult, enforce a time limit. This will teach the campers to stay calm when working against a deadline.

The Goal

The Silent Line will teach the campers to communicate with their bodies and to work with others as a team.

How to Play

Once the rules of the game are explained, the leader will call off a requirement. For example, "Line up by height or number of siblings." Start with easier requirements that can be performed with limited communication, such as height, and work up to harder requirements, such as number of siblings or smallest to largest.

For the first round, it is best to start with something easy without a time limit. As you play additional rounds, add a time limit and harder requirements.

Suggestions

Use a very tight time limit on subsequent rounds. This teaches how to work under pressure as a team.

Example Requirements

- Age (if there is a wide range of ages in the group)
- Number of siblings
- Height
- Eye color (This requirement is more difficult because the campers must look into each other's eyes to get lined up. So, make sure to give them extra time.)
- Shoe size (smallest to largest)
- Shorts length (longest to shortest assuming they are all wearing shorts)

Post-Game Questions

- Was it difficult working against a shorter deadline than you needed?

- Other than talking, what are some ways we can communicate with each other?
- How important is it that leaders be clear when they communicate?

Additional Thoughts

Too often people rely on their voice alone to convey the message they are trying to relay. There are so many other ways to communicate with your body. Hopefully, this activity helps campers think of other ways to use their bodies to communicate with others.

Photo Finish

Photo Finish sounds easy. Using tape, draw a straight line on the ground. That is the finish line. The team races to the finish line but must cross the line together at the same time. Getting a group of people to move as one takes teamwork. This game can give you a good idea of who are the natural leaders in the group.

How to Play

Have the campers line up on one side of the straight line and tell them when you say "go" they must race but also all cross the line at the same moment and touch the ground on the other side together. Take a photo or video to determine success.

Some campers will move faster than others, and on video or with a photo it becomes clear.

Suggestions

This game works best only once per group of campers.

Post-Game Questions

- Was this game harder than you thought it would be? Why?
- What did each member need to do to move across the line at the same time?
- What are some ways you can get a group to work together as one?

Additional Thoughts

Sometimes, something as easy as stepping across the line becomes difficult when you do it as a group. Good leaders need to learn how they can get their team to work as one to complete the tasks needed.

The Puzzle

Campers must compete to put a section of a puzzle together first on their own and then the complete puzzle as a team. This game teaches communication and teamwork and is an effective activity once campers get to know each other. The Puzzle also teaches the importance of every role, every member of a team. Each member is needed to complete the final product.

How to Play

Before the day of the activity, put together the puzzle you want the campers to assemble. Once you know it is a complete puzzle, break it into sections based on the number of people playing and put each section as pieces into bags. Make sure the pieces that go into each bag are all for the same area of the puzzle.

Give each camper a bag with puzzle pieces. Set two alarms. One for five minutes and tell them to put together their pieces. The second timer is for twenty minutes. When done with their part, they must work with others to put the entire puzzle together within the twenty-minute time limit. Make sure the time limit is reasonable to the size of the puzzle you are working with but make it tight enough that they feel pressure.

Suggestions

It may be best to do the exercise with a few friends first to find out how long it should take depending on the size of the group and difficulty of the puzzle.

Post-Game Questions

- Was it harder than you thought to put the puzzle sections together with the whole group? Why?
- Each member of a team must do their own part before attempting to fit the whole puzzle together. Give an example of a time when you

worked in a team where each member had to do their own part before the team could complete their task.

- What skills challenged you during this game?

Additional Thoughts

As with many things in life—every member in a company, school, or team must do their own part for everything to work. Sometimes it takes thousands of people working on their own tasks to achieve a larger goal. Without each person doing their part, the puzzle would never be complete in time. This is the same as it is for many organizations. Everyone needs to do their part. For example, consider camp. If we removed the support staff like the cooks, maintenance staff, or the administrators, how quickly do you think things would fall apart?

Egg Drop

Egg Drop is a classic activity played at camps around the world. For team building and leadership training it is best to have everyone work on one or two contraptions together.

The Goal

The goal is to teach problem solving and teamwork. You can also teach leadership by assigning a youth leader to the project to give a camper real leadership experience.

How to Play

Teams will receive one or more raw eggs, which they need to protect. Each team needs to build a contraption that will protect the egg when dropped from a significant height. You can supply the campers with items, or you can have them collect items on their own to make the device. Egg Drop can be played as one large group or with campers divided into smaller teams. Typically, the game works best with four or more youth per team.

Suggestions

Assign a leader or leaders to give them real leadership experience. Or you can have the campers work as teams without an assigned leader.

Make sure the time limit is reasonable, but some extra pressure of a tight time limit can help teens learn to deal with the stress that comes from real-life work deadlines.

Post-Game Questions

- Did your contraption work like you thought it would? Often the most important part of being a leader is the ability to look at what happened and figure out why it worked or why it failed.
- What would you change if you had to do it again?
- What skills did you use in this game?
- What skills do you need to work on?

Additional Thoughts

If you set a tight time limit, consider talking to your campers about the stress of a deadline. How often in life do you run out of time to complete a task the way you want to, so you need to decide what needs to be accomplished first. Also address the importance of taking ideas from everyone, especially if it is a task you are not expert in.

Something Changed

You can learn to be aware of your surroundings. This activity is a fun skill building activity.

The Goal

Being aware of what is happening around you is a skill to be learned and developed. Campers will become more aware of the importance of paying attention to their surroundings.

How to Play

Divide the campers into two groups: Team A and Team B. Have the two teams line up facing each other about ten feet apart. Tell Team A to carefully look at Team B. Send Team A into a different room where they cannot see or hear Team B. Team B needs to make one change to the lineup. Once that is done, call in Team A and ask them to spot the difference in the Team B line. Have the teams take turns until you run out of time.

Suggestions

Let the campers decide what to change. It must be something that can be seen easily from ten feet away. Act as a judge to keep the game fair and fun. An idea could be campers switching shirts.

Post-Game Questions

- How did you do as an individual? Leaders need to first look at themselves before they look at what went wrong with the team.
- How did you do as a team? Leaders need to give an honest look at how their team did without any type of personal attachment clouding their thoughts.
- What did you learn from this game?

Additional Thoughts

Ask your campers to identify times that being aware of what is happening around them is important. Use examples like the importance of noticing a camper that is suddenly not with the group, walking in a dark parking lot, or going to a bank machine. Talk to them about how being aware of their surroundings is a skill that can be developed with practice. If you have any suggestions, give them tips on how to be aware of the activities around you.

I Am Leader

With the I Am Leader game, you can help campers find their natural leadership skills. Campers take a deep look at themselves as a leader in an honest way.

How to Play

Ask campers to line up facing you on the other side of the room. Next, read out a list of statements that describe a leader, such as "I am able to make decisions even when I am stressed" or "I am comfortable making important decisions." If the answer is yes, the camper will take a large step forward. Every time a camper steps forward ask them to explain why they think they have the skill read out.

Suggested Statements

- I am a natural leader.
- I accept responsibility for my actions no matter what.
- I have learned how to handle stress in my everyday life.
- I have a positive attitude even when things are not going my way.
- I can make important decisions when I have all the time I need to think about it.
- I can make important decisions when time is limited and a decision is needed right now.
- I do not blame others when things go wrong.
- My goal is to become a great leader.
- My goal is to help others become better people.
- I put others first at work.
- I put others first at home.

Post-Game Questions

- What statement made you think twice before you answered?
- What skill do you think you need to work on most?
- Which skill do you think was most important?

Additional Thoughts

This game will give campers a moment to think about themselves in an honest and fun way. Often the best way to get people to open up is to have them move around. When seated its tempting to stay quiet, but when they move they are far more likely to talk and open up.

Balls & Buckets

This is an exciting game to get campers to think creatively and to work together.

The Goal

The goal is to get the campers to work together to creatively problem solve.

How to Play

Divide the campers into at least two teams. Set up two buckets ten feet apart for each team. The campers must move the balls from one bucket to the other without using their hands or arms.

Note: Campers cannot move the buckets, and if the buckets get knocked over the campers must stop and put everything back without their hands or arms losing time as the other team keeps moving. The goal is to find objects or ways to move the balls without touching them with their hands.

Suggestions

Another way to play the game is for each team to have a handler. The handler is one person who can touch the balls once they are out of the bucket to move them to the other bucket. The handler cannot remove balls from the bucket. Having a handler teaches campers delegation.

Consider setting a time limit to add extra pressure and excitement to the game.

Post-Game Questions

- What strategies or processes did you use to overcome the problem?
- Was it hard to trust one person with the role of the handler? Why?
- What skill did you excel at in this game?

Additional Thoughts

With this game, campers are forced to think creatively. There is a seemingly easy task to complete but the lack of their hands suddenly makes it difficult. Often in life a task that can seem easy becomes hard because you are limited in some way. Leaders need to overcome this by thinking creatively.

Scavenger Hunt

This Scavenger Hunt is a classic game with a twist. Instead of just giving campers hints on where to go next, give the players activities at each spot to do as a team to earn the next hint. You can split the group into teams to race each other or offer a prize if they complete the Scavenger Hunt within the time limit.

The Goal

With the Scavenger Hunt campers are moving and thinking both as a leader and as a team. By physically having to work together to complete the Scavenger Hunt they will learn more than a traditional classroom can teach.

How to Play

You can break campers up into small groups or have them do it as a large group. Create multiple locations for your adventure that will require your campers to work as a team to complete an objective to get a clue to the next location. The number of locations and how long the activities take can change depending on how much time you spend on this project. The campers work together to complete the course as quickly as possible.

Suggested Activities

There are numerous short activities that can be performed at each stage of the hunt. The following are a few examples:

- Put together a small puzzle.
- Unscramble a phrase.
- Answer questions about leadership.
- Complete a simple team exercise like human knot or team jump rope.

Post-Game Questions

- What was the hardest part of completing these activities as a team?
- What changes do you wish you could have made?
- How important is reviewing your work during the game?

Additional Thoughts

Your goal is to get campers outside of the classroom setting and have them learn to work as a team out in the world. Give as little help as you can get away with as we hope this will build confidence in themselves and their abilities.

Leading the Blind

This is a fun game where one camper is blindfolded, and their teammates must talk them through a maze.

The Goal

Leading the Blind teaches communication skills and the importance of clear instructions.

How to Play

This game is as simple or as hard as you want to make it. One person will be blindfolded, and the rest of the campers will try to talk them through the maze. This game is best played on a flat surface with a tape maze on the ground. Avoid using chairs and other objects that campers can trip over. Ensure an adult is supervising the game to make sure everyone is playing safely.

Leading the Blind can be played as one group or by dividing campers into teams.

Suggestions

When you blindfold the camper, do it away from the starting line, then walk them to the starting line. By doing so, you avoid campers memorizing the maze beforehand.

Consider setting a time limit to add some pressure to the game.

Post-Game Questions

- What was the toughest part of being the person who was blindfolded?
- What was the toughest part of being the team trying to guide the blindfolded person through the maze?
- Was it harder to communicate what you wanted the blindfolded person to do than you thought it would be? Why?

Additional Thoughts

As the game unfolds, remember to point out the importance of clear communication. Too often when too many people are talking at the same time it can be hard for team members to understand what is wanted from them.

Ball Maze

The ball maze offers a fun way to force campers to work together as they try to maneuver golf or tennis balls through a maze created from a bed sheet that you cut some holes into.

The Goal

To see what others are doing and to talk and listen to work together to score the most goals.

How to Play

Take a large bed sheet and cut some random holes in it. Draw a goal on one part of the sheet. In teams or as a group, campers each pull a part of the sheet to make it tight. Place a golf ball or a tennis ball in the center of the sheet. The campers must work together to move the ball into the goal.

Suggestions

Make sure you do not overdo it with the holes. This should be hard but not impossible.

Post-Game Questions

- What was the hardest part of this game?
- How did you end up winning?
- What did you learn about teamwork?

Additional Thoughts

Like in the game of life you often have a group of people all pulling in different directions. A leader needs to find a way to get all of the team members to work together to reach the goal.

Team Jump Rope

This is a quick fun game to get campers moving and working as a team. All you need is a long rope and a group of kids.

The Goal

To get kids talking and thinking as a team to problem solve.

How to Play

Two campers swing a long rope as a group of campers attempts to jump over the rope together. This will force them as a team to start communicating and working together.

Post-Game Questions

- What was the hardest part of the game?
- If one person refused to work as a team could you complete this game?
- What would make this game easier?

Additional Thoughts

Sometimes the simplest task can become hard in a group. Jumping rope is not a difficult task but getting everyone to move at the same pace can be. A leader must learn to get their team working together as one to achieve their goals.

Sit Down Activities

Sometimes you just need to sit down and do an activity to get your campers thinking.

What Leaders Do You Respect?

For this activity, ask campers to tell the group the name(s) of a leader(s) they respect and why.

The Goal

This starts an open-ended discussion about what it means to be a leader that others respect and, more importantly, follow.

How to Play

This activity works best if you have a large piece of paper or a white board to write the responses on. Get as many names of leaders as possible. Make sure to follow it up with the post-game questions to get them thinking and talking.

Post-Game Questions

- What do these leaders have in common?
- What other reasons make you like a leader?
- Is it important for you to like a leader for you to follow them?
- What can we learn from them?

Additional Thoughts

Make sure to direct the conversation toward what makes a good leader and how they can obtain these qualities. This is a perfect opportunity to talk about being the leader people want to follow and how to do that.

Team Logo

This is a great activity for a team to create a logo, flag, or emblem that will represent their team during their CIT/LIT year.

The Goal

Logos, flags, and emblems have meanings and can rally people to a cause or a movement. During this activity, all the campers must work together to create a logo, flag, or emblem, and that item must have some meaning behind it for the group that is clearly shown.

How to Play

Supply the campers with the materials needed to make a logo, flag, or emblem. (Markers, paper, fabric, scissors, paint, dowels, and more.) Require them to all agree on the idea and have them write down a short explanation of what the meaning behind the logo is and how it is something they will rally behind during their CIT/LIT year.

Post-Game Questions

- What logos, flags, emblems do you see every day that rally people together?
- How could you use this at a company, school, or with a team to get people to work together?
- How do you think you can use the power of a logo, flag, or emblem in your life?

Additional Thoughts

People like to rally around something they can see. A logo, flag, or emblem has a lot of power. It can create instant bonds between strangers breaking down boundaries that otherwise would be there.

What If?

This is a great game to play with campers late in the leadership training program.

The Goal

To role play real-life scenarios to practice the leadership skills needed to solve certain problems.

How to Play

In this activity, the campers are given scenarios that a manager/leader would likely address. The campers get to create solutions to real life scenarios as a team. Campers take what they have learned in small groups and come up with ideas on how to address these situations. Adding a time limit can give more of a real-life work feel to dealing with problems. The campers must use what they learned to solve the problems and explain what skills they learned that helped them come up with a solution to the problems presented to them.

Suggestions

Activities like this work best when the campers have some idea about the task they will overcome. Consider using activities like what is happening at camp to come up with the problems they need to solve.

Example Projects

- The food truck was delayed and the planned food for tonight's dinner will not be here in time. How can we ensure a dinner will be provided to the campers?
- Several staff came down sick and you do not have enough staff to run some of the activities. There are thirty campers left without staff for their activities for an hour. What would you do to ensure the campers are not only supervised but also have something to do?
- The day before camp started a severe storm hit camp that damaged the dining room to the point that it cannot be used, and all power has been lost at camp for at least a week. What would you do?

Post-Game Questions

- How did you use what you learned in camp to handle the problem?
- What did you think would be the toughest part of being a leader when issues like this come up?
- What skill that was utilized in this game did you excel at?
- What skill could you work on?

Additional Thoughts

There is only so much people can learn from a lecture. We must get campers minds moving with games like this. Giving them an opportunity to build on what they have learned helps them become great leaders.

What Makes a Great Leader?

Have you ever thought about what makes a great leader? This is a good activity to do early on with your campers. Have them sit down and, as a group, write out what it means to be a great leader. What values does a great leader possess? What skills are needed?

The Goal

To define what a great leader is as a group.

How to Play

This game works best if the answers are written down on a white board or on a large piece of paper. If you can, use paper to save the answers and hang them in the room. Get the conversation started but try to get the campers to think about what they perceive as a strong leader.

Post-Game Questions

- When looking at the list, what stands out most to you?
- What do you think is the least important qualification of being a leader?
- What quality or skill from this list do you need to work on?
- What quality or skill do you excel at?

Additional Thoughts

What makes a great leader can mean different things to different people. Seeing other people's expectations of a leader can be an eye-opening experience. Use this activity to open the campers' eyes to different perspectives.

This or That?

Present a scenario that the campers must overcome. After they know the project, present them with a group of objects that could help them with the task or scenario. The campers must decide as a group which objects to take and which objects to leave behind. They must also explain why they picked the objects they did and why they left behind what they did.

The Goal

This is an effective exercise to teach campers that sometimes you will not have all the tools you need when facing life's problems. Also, sometimes you must make difficult decisions.

How to Play

This or That? can be played as a large group or several small teams. (The groups often end up with different answers to the same problems.) To play, first gather a group of objects that could be helpful for campers when faced with a situation. Present the campers with a project they need to complete. Next, present campers with a group of objects that could help them with the task or scenario. The campers must decide as a group which objects to take and which objects to leave behind. All the objects are helpful, but they can only use a few of them. They must also explain why they picked the objects they did and why they left behind what they did. Make sure to put a time limit on this game so you can have multiple rounds.

Suggestions

Example problems: staffing, location, maybe only enough staff to do one job but you have multiple people all needing work done at the same time. This activity helps campers learn to focus on what is important.

Post-Game Questions

- What was the hardest part of deciding what to leave behind?
- At what points in life and work do you think you will be forced to complete a task when you do not have all the tools you want or need?
- As a leader, at what times do you think you will be forced into a situation like this?

Additional Thoughts

With this activity we try to get campers to think about what is important. Often as a leader you do not have the time or the ability to do everything you want. At some point you need to pick what is most important.

The No Hands Cup Stack

Campers must stack cups as high as they can without touching them.

The Goal

The No Hands Cup Stack game forces each camper to do their part. If one person fails to work as a team the game will not work.

How to Play

Give each team a rubber band with four or more ropes coming off the corners. Each camper takes a rope. The campers must work together to pick up cups and move them to the assigned location stacking the cups as high as possible within a time limit.

Suggestions

Make sure the rubber bands are large enough to go over the cups but not too loose that they cannot hold the cups.

Post-Game Questions

- How important was your role?
- If you did not do your part could your team win? Why?
- What skill did you learn in this game?

Additional Thoughts

Sometimes even when your part seems small if you do not do it the whole project cannot be completed.

Jelly Beans

With this game campers must make deals with other campers to get all the same color jelly beans.

The Goal

The goal is to teach campers to negotiate with others to get what they need. To complete a task, we must work with others to get what they have for our projects.

How to Play

Give each camper the same number of jelly beans as there are campers in the group. Once each camper has their beans, they must trade with others to obtain all the same color jelly beans. To do this, players must make deals and communicate as a leader.

Post-Game Questions

- How did you do?
- What skills did you excel at?
- What skills can you work on?

Additional Thoughts

Often when we have projects to complete, we need the skills of others. What are good ways to get people to be willing to help you or give you the skills and/or items you need?

Point of View

With this activity you ask the campers to describe themselves in the third person.

The Goal

The goal of this activity is to get campers to take an honest look at themselves by forcing them to talk about themselves from others point of view.

How to Play

Start by asking the campers to describe themselves as others would. What do you look like from others point of view? How do others see you as a person? How would they describe you? This game forces campers to look at themselves from the point of view of those around them.

Suggestions

This game works best if the leader goes first and gives an example of how it works.

Post-Game Questions

- The first question is for the campers to think about not publicly answer. Are you happy with how others see you? If not, what would you change?
- How do you want others to perceive you?
- What skills did you learn in this game?

Additional Thoughts

This activity will force campers outside of their comfort zone. It is valuable for them to think differently and openly about what is happening to them. To do this sometimes you have to look at yourself from the point of view of others.

Closing Thoughts & Tips

You now have a blueprint to run your CIT/LIT program. I do want to take a quick moment and give you as the leader a few final ideas and thoughts.

Do What Is Right for You…

This book lays out ideas to help you get started but only you know what is right for you and your program. Take these ideas and use them how you see fit. Don't feel that you need to do everything exactly the way the book lays it out. Though I would encourage you to try to take as many of these ideas as you can I do understand they may not always be the right fit for you.

Take Care of Yourself

As a leader of your CIT/LIT program make sure you take time to take care of yourself. Burn out is very easy at summer camps especially at overnight camps. You can easily find yourself working 24/7 and skipping time off. Make sure you take the time needed to focus on yourself and your mental health so you can give your campers 100% every day.

Remember the Final Goal

The final goal of your program should be twofold. First, to help make your campers into better adults when they grow up. Second, to give them the skills they need to succeed at life.

You have a great opportunity to make a lasting impact on your campers not just now but for the rest of their life. That may sound scary but it's also a great opportunity to make a lasting impact on the future of your community through your campers.

Avoid the Temptation to Make This Just About Camp

That may seem weird considering this program is made for summer camps. Yet remember that we are not just trying to train future camp counselors but also trying to give the campers skills they need in life. So make sure you are not just training your campers as counselors for your camp but giving them real world skills they will need in life.

A few ideas on how to use your CIT/LIT program to help you find camp staff.

I may have just talked about not making this all about your camp but let's talk about a few ways to get CITs/LITs to come back as staff in the years to come. Here are a few ways to convince them to come and work with you at camp again.

Don't Abuse Your CITs/LITs

One of the main reasons CITs and LITs don't come back is because they feel like forced labor that was not paid at camp. Make sure you remember that CITs and LITs are not staff. Many camps work them like staff but don't give them days off or pay. Avoid the temptation to treat campers as staff even when they are CITs/LITs.

Make the Offer

Often camps just send their CITs/LITs home and hope they apply to be staff next year. Before they go home make sure to take a moment and ask them to think about coming back as paid staff. Make that offer again after they go home in writing. Don't guarantee them a job but make the request that they apply as staff. This will allow you to still turn down some you don't want but hopefully get a few of the good ones to come back as staff.

Consider Making Them a Special Offer

Some of the best staff you can get are staff that used to be campers. Consider offering them an opportunity to maybe become full staff instead of junior staff. Or maybe offer them a small pay bonus if they completed the CIT/LIT program before becoming staff. This can also help attract campers to your CIT/LIT program.

A small bonus may be skipping the junior staff year or a slight pay bonus. Either can help you attract some of your best campers to become staff.

Let Us Know How the Program Worked for You

As you go through this program please take notes and let us know what worked for you and what did not. Your feedback helps us improve this program and hopefully help camps around the world. You can send your feedback to Feedback@BeechtreeAssets.com.

Closing Thoughts

I hope this book has helped you build a great program for your CIT/LITs. This program can be one of the most important programs your camp runs, and we hope that this helped you take your program to the next level.

A strong CIT/LIT program can help you attract campers to your camp that maybe never attended your camp before.

Lastly, always remember:
The leader has to be practical and a realist yet must talk the language of the visionary and the idealist. —Eric Hoffer